CHILD CUSTOD

MW01234864

THIS BOOK BELONGS TO:	
Name	
Address	
Email	
Tel.	

LOG BOOK DETAILS	
Start date	
Number	

Visit details			
Date			
Weekday			
Pick up time		Agreed pick up time	
Drop off time		Agreed drop off time	
Child's name			
Child's age			
Location			

Special requirements

Custodian's details	
Name	
Relationship to child	
Address	
Email	
Tel. no.	
Signature	

Notes

Visit details		
Date		
Weekday		
Pick up time	Agreed pick up time	
Drop off time	Agreed drop off time	
Child's name		
Child's age		
Location		

Special requirements

Custodian's details
Name	
Relationship to child	
Address	
Email	
Tel. no.	
Signature	

Notes

Visit details

Date			
Weekday			
Pick up time		Agreed pick up time	
Drop off time		Agreed drop off time	
Child's name			
Child's age			
Location			

Special requirements

Custodian's details

Name	
Relationship to child	
Address	
Email	
Tel. no.	
Signature	

Notes

Visit details			
Date			
Weekday			
Pick up time		Agreed pick up time	
Drop off time		Agreed drop off time	
Child's name			
Child's age			
Location			

Special requirements

Custodian's details	
Name	
Relationship to child	
Address	
Email	
Tel. no.	
Signature	

Notes

Visit details			
Date			
Weekday			
Pick up time		Agreed pick up time	
Drop off tlme		Agreed drop off tlme	
Child's name			
Child's age			
Location			

Special requirements

Custodian's details	
Name	
Relationship to child	
Address	
Email	
Tel. no.	
Signature	

Notes

Visit details		
Date		
Weekday		
Pick up time	Agreed pick up time	
Drop off time	Agreed drop off time	
Child's name		
Child's age		
Location		

Special requirements

Custodian's details	
Name	
Relationship to child	
Address	
Email	
Tel. no.	
Signature	

Notes

Visit details	
Date	
Weekday	

Pick up time		Agreed pick up time	
Drop off time		Agreed drop off time	

Child's name	
Child's age	
Location	

Special requirements	

Custodian's details	
Name	
Relationship to child	
Address	
Email	
Tel. no.	
Signature	

Notes	

Visit details			
Date			
Weekday			
Pick up time		Agreed pick up time	
Drop off time		Agreed drop off time	
Child's name			
Child's age			
Location			

Special requirements

Custodian's details	
Name	
Relationship to child	
Address	
Email	
Tel. no.	
Signature	

Notes

Visit details		
Date		
Weekday		
Pick up time	Agreed pick up time	
Drop off time	Agreed drop off time	
Child's name		
Child's age		
Location		

Special requirements

Custodian's details	
Name	
Relationship to child	
Address	
Email	
Tel. no.	
Signature	

Notes

Visit details	
Date	
Weekday	
Pick up time	Agreed pick up time	
Drop off time	Agreed drop off time	
Child's name	
Child's age	
Location	

Special requirements

Custodian's details	
Name	
Relationship to child	
Address	
Email	
Tel. no.	
Signature	

Notes

Visit details			
Date			
Weekday			
Pick up time		Agreed pick up time	
Drop off time		Agreed drop off time	
Child's name			
Child's age			
Location			

Special requirements

Custodian's details	
Name	
Relationship to child	
Address	
Email	
Tel. no.	
Signature	

Notes

Visit details	
Date	
Weekday	
Pick up time	Agreed pick up time
Drop off time	Agreed drop off time
Child's name	
Child's age	
Location	

Special requirements

Custodian's details

Name	
Relationship to child	
Address	
Email	
Tel. no.	
Signature	

Notes

Visit details		
Date		
Weekday		
Pick up time	Agreed pick up time	
Drop off time	Agreed drop off time	
Child's name		
Child's age		
Location		

Special requirements

Custodian's details	
Name	
Relationship to child	
Address	
Email	
Tel. no.	
Signature	

Notes

Visit details			
Date			
Weekday			
Pick up time		Agreed pick up time	
Drop off time		Agreed drop off time	
Child's name			
Child's age			
Location			

Special requirements

Custodian's details	
Name	
Relationship to child	
Address	
Email	
Tel. no.	
Signature	

Notes

Visit details

Date			
Weekday			
Pick up time		Agreed pick up time	
Drop off time		Agreed drop off time	
Child's name			
Child's age			
Location			

Special requirements

Custodian's details

Name	
Relationship to child	
Address	
Email	
Tel. no.	
Signature	

Notes

Visit details		
Date		
Weekday		
Pick up time	Agreed pick up time	
Drop off time	Agreed drop off time	
Child's name		
Child's age		
Location		

Special requirements

Custodian's details	
Name	
Relationship to child	
Address	
Email	
Tel. no.	
Signature	

Notes

Visit details

Date	
Weekday	
Pick up time	Agreed pick up time
Drop off time	Agreed drop off time
Child's name	
Child's age	
Location	

Special requirements

Custodian's details

Name	
Relationship to child	
Address	
Email	
Tel. no.	
Signature	

Notes

Visit details		
Date		
Weekday		
Pick up time	Agreed pick up time	
Drop off time	Agreed drop off time	
Child's name		
Child's age		
Location		

Special requirements

Custodian's details	
Name	
Relationship to child	
Address	
Email	
Tel. no.	
Signature	

Notes

Visit details			
Date			
Weekday			
Pick up time		Agreed pick up time	
Drop off time		Agreed drop off time	
Child's name			
Child's age			
Location			

Special requirements

Custodian's details	
Name	
Relationship to child	
Address	
Email	
Tel. no.	
Signature	

Notes

Visit details		
Date		
Weekday		
Pick up time		Agreed pick up time
Drop off time		Agreed drop off time
Child's name		
Child's age		
Location		

Special requirements

Custodian's details	
Name	
Relationship to child	
Address	
Email	
Tel. no.	
Signature	

Notes

Visit details		
Date		
Weekday		
Pick up time		Agreed pick up time	
Drop off time		Agreed drop off time	
Child's name		
Child's age		
Location		

Special requirements

Custodian's details	
Name	
Relationship to child	
Address	
Email	
Tel. no.	
Signature	

Notes

Visit details		
Date		
Weekday		
Pick up time	Agreed pick up time	
Drop off time	Agreed drop off time	
Child's name		
Child's age		
Location		

Special requirements

Custodian's details	
Name	
Relationship to child	
Address	
Email	
Tel. no.	
Signature	

Notes

Visit details			
Date			
Weekday			
Pick up time		Agreed pick up time	
Drop off time		Agreed drop off time	
Child's name			
Child's age			
Location			

Special requirements

Custodian's details	
Name	
Relationship to child	
Address	
Email	
Tel. no.	
Signature	

Notes

Visit details			
Date			
Weekday			
Pick up time		Agreed pick up time	
Drop off time		Agreed drop off time	
Child's name			
Child's age			
Location			

Special requirements

Custodian's details	
Name	
Relationship to child	
Address	
Email	
Tel. no.	
Signature	

Notes

Visit details		
Date		
Weekday		
Pick up time	Agreed pick up time	
Drop off time	Agreed drop off time	
Child's name		
Child's age		
Location		

Special requirements

Custodian's details	
Name	
Relationship to child	
Address	
Email	
Tel. no.	
Signature	

Notes

Visit details			
Date			
Weekday			
Pick up time		Agreed pick up time	
Drop off time		Agreed drop off time	
Child's name			
Child's age			
Location			

Special requirements

Custodian's details	
Name	
Relationship to child	
Address	
Email	
Tel. no.	
Signature	

Notes

Visit details			
Date			
Weekday			
Pick up time		Agreed pick up time	
Drop off time		Agreed drop off time	
Child's name			
Child's age			
Location			

Special requirements

Custodian's details	
Name	
Relationship to child	
Address	
Email	
Tel. no.	
Signature	

Notes

Visit details

Date	
Weekday	
Pick up time	Agreed pick up time	
Drop off time	Agreed drop off time	
Child's name	
Child's age	
Location	

Special requirements

Custodian's details

Name	
Relationship to child	
Address	
Email	
Tel. no.	
Signature	

Notes

Visit details			
Date			
Weekday			
Pick up time		Agreed pick up time	
Drop off time		Agreed drop off time	
Child's name			
Child's age			
Location			

Special requirements

Custodian's details	
Name	
Relationship to child	
Address	
Email	
Tel. no.	
Signature	

Notes

Visit details		
Date		
Weekday		
Pick up time	Agreed pick up time	
Drop off time	Agreed drop off time	
Child's name		
Child's age		
Location		

Special requirements

Custodian's details	
Name	
Relationship to child	
Address	
Email	
Tel. no.	
Signature	

Notes

Visit details		
Date		
Weekday		
Pick up time	Agreed pick up time	
Drop off time	Agreed drop off time	
Child's name		
Child's age		
Location		

Special requirements

Custodian's details	
Name	
Relationship to child	
Address	
Email	
Tel. no.	
Signature	

Notes

Visit details		
Date		
Weekday		
Pick up time	Agreed pick up time	
Drop off time	Agreed drop off time	
Child's name		
Child's age		
Location		

Special requirements

Custodian's details	
Name	
Relationship to child	
Address	
Email	
Tel. no.	
Signature	

Notes

Visit details			
Date			
Weekday			
Pick up time		Agreed pick up time	
Drop off time		Agreed drop off time	
Child's name			
Child's age			
Location			

Special requirements

Custodian's details	
Name	
Relationship to child	
Address	
Email	
Tel. no.	
Signature	

Notes

Visit details	
Date	
Weekday	
Pick up time	Agreed pick up time	
Drop off time	Agreed drop off time	
Child's name	
Child's age	
Location	

Special requirements

Custodian's details	
Name	
Relationship to child	
Address	
Email	
Tel. no.	
Signature	

Notes

Visit details	
Date	
Weekday	
Pick up time	Agreed pick up time
Drop off time	Agreed drop off time
Child's name	
Child's age	
Location	

Special requirements

Custodian's details	
Name	
Relationship to child	
Address	
Email	
Tel. no.	
Signature	

Notes

Visit details			
Date			
Weekday			
Pick up time		Agreed pick up time	
Drop off time		Agreed drop off time	
Child's name			
Child's age			
Location			

Special requirements

Custodian's details	
Name	
Relationship to child	
Address	
Email	
Tel. no.	
Signature	

Notes

Visit details		
Date		
Weekday		
Pick up time		Agreed pick up time	
Drop off time		Agreed drop off time	
Child's name		
Child's age		
Location		

Special requirements

Custodian's details	
Name	
Relationship to child	
Address	
Email	
Tel. no.	
Signature	

Notes

Visit details			
Date			
Weekday			
Pick up time		Agreed pick up time	
Drop off time		Agreed drop off time	
Child's name			
Child's age			
Location			

Special requirements

Custodian's details	
Name	
Relationship to child	
Address	
Email	
Tel. no.	
Signature	

Notes

Visit details			
Date			
Weekday			
Pick up time		Agreed pick up time	
Drop off time		Agreed drop off time	
Child's name			
Child's age			
Location			

Special requirements

Custodian's details	
Name	
Relationship to child	
Address	
Email	
Tel. no.	
Signature	

Notes

Visit details			
Date			
Weekday			
Pick up time		Agreed pick up time	
Drop off time		Agreed drop off time	
Child's name			
Child's age			
Location			

Special requirements

Custodian's details	
Name	
Relationship to child	
Address	
Email	
Tel. no.	
Signature	

Notes

Visit details			
Date			
Weekday			
Pick up time		Agreed pick up time	
Drop off time		Agreed drop off time	
Child's name			
Child's age			
Location			

Special requirements

Custodian's details	
Name	
Relationship to child	
Address	
Email	
Tel. no.	
Signature	

Notes

Visit details			
Date			
Weekday			
Pick up time		Agreed pick up time	
Drop off time		Agreed drop off time	
Child's name			
Child's age			
Location			

Special requirements

Custodian's details	
Name	
Relationship to child	
Address	
Email	
Tel. no.	
Signature	

Notes

Visit details		
Date		
Weekday		
Pick up time		Agreed pick up time	
Drop off time		Agreed drop off time	
Child's name		
Child's age		
Location		

Special requirements

Custodian's details	
Name	
Relationship to child	
Address	
Email	
Tel. no.	
Signature	

Notes

Visit details			
Date			
Weekday			
Pick up time		Agreed pick up time	
Drop off time		Agreed drop off time	
Child's name			
Child's age			
Location			

Special requirements

Custodian's details	
Name	
Relationship to child	
Address	
Email	
Tel. no.	
Signature	

Notes

Visit details

Date	
Weekday	

		Agreed pick up time	
Pick up time		Agreed pick up time	
Drop off time		Agreed drop off time	

Child's name	
Child's age	
Location	

Special requirements

Custodian's details

Name	
Relationship to child	
Address	
Email	
Tel. no.	
Signature	

Notes

Visit details		
Date		
Weekday		
Pick up time	Agreed pick up time	
Drop off time	Agreed drop off time	
Child's name		
Child's age		
Location		

Special requirements

Custodian's details	
Name	
Relationship to child	
Address	
Email	
Tel. no.	
Signature	

Notes

Visit details		
Date		
Weekday		
Pick up time		Agreed pick up time	
Drop off time		Agreed drop off time	
Child's name		
Child's age		
Location		

Special requirements

Custodian's details	
Name	
Relationship to child	
Address	
Email	
Tel. no.	
Signature	

Notes

Visit details			
Date			
Weekday			
Pick up time		Agreed pick up time	
Drop off time		Agreed drop off time	
Child's name			
Child's age			
Location			

Special requirements

Custodian's details	
Name	
Relationship to child	
Address	
Email	
Tel. no.	
Signature	

Notes

Visit details			
Date			
Weekday			
Pick up time		Agreed pick up time	
Drop off time		Agreed drop off time	
Child's name			
Child's age			
Location			

Special requirements

Custodian's details	
Name	
Relationship to child	
Address	
Email	
Tel. no.	
Signature	

Notes

Visit details		
Date		
Weekday		
Pick up time	Agreed pick up time	
Drop off time	Agreed drop off time	
Child's name		
Child's age		
Location		

Special requirements

Custodian's details	
Name	
Relationship to child	
Address	
Email	
Tel. no.	
Signature	

Notes

Visit details		
Date		
Weekday		
Pick up time	Agreed pick up time	
Drop off time	Agreed drop off time	
Child's name		
Child's age		
Location		

Special requirements

Custodian's details	
Name	
Relationship to child	
Address	
Email	
Tel. no.	
Signature	

Notes

Visit details	
Date	
Weekday	
Pick up time	Agreed pick up time
Drop off time	Agreed drop off time
Child's name	
Child's age	
Location	

Special requirements

Custodian's details	
Name	
Relationship to child	
Address	
Email	
Tel. no.	
Signature	

Notes

Visit details			
Date			
Weekday			
Pick up time		Agreed pick up time	
Drop off time		Agreed drop off time	
Child's name			
Child's age			
Location			

Special requirements

Custodian's details	
Name	
Relationship to child	
Address	
Email	
Tel. no.	
Signature	

Notes

Visit details			
Date			
Weekday			
Pick up time		Agreed pick up time	
Drop off time		Agreed drop off time	
Child's name			
Child's age			
Location			

Special requirements

Custodian's details	
Name	
Relationship to child	
Address	
Email	
Tel. no.	
Signature	

Notes

Visit details			
Date			
Weekday			
Pick up time		Agreed pick up time	
Drop off time		Agreed drop off time	
Child's name			
Child's age			
Location			

Special requirements

Custodian's details	
Name	
Relationship to child	
Address	
Email	
Tel. no.	
Signature	

Notes

Visit details		
Date		
Weekday		
Pick up time	Agreed pick up time	
Drop off time	Agreed drop off time	
Child's name		
Child's age		
Location		

Special requirements

Custodian's details	
Name	
Relationship to child	
Address	
Email	
Tel. no.	
Signature	

Notes

Visit details			
Date			
Weekday			
Pick up time		Agreed pick up time	
Drop off time		Agreed drop off time	
Child's name			
Child's age			
Location			

Special requirements

Custodian's details	
Name	
Relationship to child	
Address	
Email	
Tel. no.	
Signature	

Notes

Visit details		
Date		
Weekday		
Pick up time		Agreed pick up time	
Drop off time		Agreed drop off time	
Child's name		
Child's age		
Location		

Special requirements

Custodian's details	
Name	
Relationship to child	
Address	
Email	
Tel. no.	
Signature	

Notes

Visit details	
Date	
Weekday	
Pick up time	
Drop off time	
Child's name	
Child's age	
Location	

		Agreed pick up time	
		Agreed drop off time	

Special requirements

Custodian's details

Name	
Relationship to child	
Address	
Email	
Tel. no.	
Signature	

Notes

Visit details			
Date			
Weekday			
Pick up time		Agreed pick up time	
Drop off time		Agreed drop off time	
Child's name			
Child's age			
Location			

Special requirements

Custodian's details	
Name	
Relationship to child	
Address	
Email	
Tel. no.	
Signature	

Notes

Visit details			
Date			
Weekday			
Pick up time		Agreed pick up time	
Drop off time		Agreed drop off time	
Child's name			
Child's age			
Location			

Special requirements

Custodian's details	
Name	
Relationship to child	
Address	
Email	
Tel. no.	
Signature	

Notes

Visit details		
Date		
Weekday		
Pick up time	Agreed pick up time	
Drop off time	Agreed drop off time	
Child's name		
Child's age		
Location		

Special requirements

Custodian's details	
Name	
Relationship to child	
Address	
Email	
Tel. no.	
Signature	

Notes

Visit details	
Date	
Weekday	

		Agreed pick up time	
Pick up time		Agreed pick up time	
Drop off time		Agreed drop off time	

Child's name	
Child's age	
Location	

Special requirements

Custodian's details

Name	
Relationship to child	
Address	
Email	
Tel. no.	
Signature	

Notes

Visit details			
Date			
Weekday			
Pick up time		Agreed pick up time	
Drop off time		Agreed drop off time	
Child's name			
Child's age			
Location			

Special requirements

Custodian's details	
Name	
Relationship to child	
Address	
Email	
Tel. no.	
Signature	

Notes

Visit details			
Date			
Weekday			
Pick up time		Agreed pick up time	
Drop off time		Agreed drop off time	
Child's name			
Child's age			
Location			

Special requirements

Custodian's details	
Name	
Relationship to child	
Address	
Email	
Tel. no.	
Signature	

Notes

Visit details

Date	
Weekday	

Pick up time		Agreed pick up time	
Drop off time		Agreed drop off time	

Child's name	
Child's age	
Location	

Special requirements

Custodian's details

Name	
Relationship to child	
Address	
Email	
Tel. no.	
Signature	

Notes

Visit details		
Date		
Weekday		
Pick up time	Agreed pick up time	
Drop off time	Agreed drop off time	
Child's name		
Child's age		
Location		

Special requirements

Custodian's details	
Name	
Relationship to child	
Address	
Email	
Tel. no.	
Signature	

Notes

Visit details		
Date		
Weekday		
Pick up time	Agreed pick up time	
Drop off time	Agreed drop off time	
Child's name		
Child's age		
Location		

Special requirements

Custodian's details	
Name	
Relationship to child	
Address	
Email	
Tel. no.	
Signature	

Notes

Visit details		
Date		
Weekday		
Pick up time	Agreed pick up time	
Drop off time	Agreed drop off time	
Child's name		
Child's age		
Location		

Special requirements

Custodian's details	
Name	
Relationship to child	
Address	
Email	
Tel. no.	
Signature	

Notes

Visit details		
Date		
Weekday		
Pick up time		Agreed pick up time	
Drop off time		Agreed drop off time	
Child's name		
Child's age		
Location		

Special requirements

Custodian's details	
Name	
Relationship to child	
Address	
Email	
Tel. no.	
Signature	

Notes

Visit details		
Date		
Weekday		
Pick up time		Agreed pick up time	
Drop off time		Agreed drop off time	
Child's name		
Child's age		
Location		

Special requirements

Custodian's details	
Name	
Relationship to child	
Address	
Email	
Tel. no.	
Signature	

Notes

Visit details			
Date			
Weekday			
Pick up time		Agreed pick up time	
Drop off time		Agreed drop off time	
Child's name			
Child's age			
Location			

Special requirements

Custodian's details	
Name	
Relationship to child	
Address	
Email	
Tel. no.	
Signature	

Notes

Visit details		
Date		
Weekday		
Pick up time	Agreed pick up time	
Drop off time	Agreed drop off time	
Child's name		
Child's age		
Location		

Special requirements

Custodian's details	
Name	
Relationship to child	
Address	
Email	
Tel. no.	
Signature	

Notes

Visit details		
Date		
Weekday		
Pick up time	Agreed pick up time	
Drop off time	Agreed drop off time	
Child's name		
Child's age		
Location		

Special requirements

Custodian's details	
Name	
Relationship to child	
Address	
Email	
Tel. no.	
Signature	

Notes

Visit details			
Date			
Weekday			
Pick up time		Agreed pick up time	
Drop off time		Agreed drop off time	
Child's name			
Child's age			
Location			

Special requirements

Custodian's details	
Name	
Relationship to child	
Address	
Email	
Tel. no.	
Signature	

Notes

Visit details		
Date		
Weekday		
Pick up time	Agreed pick up time	
Drop off time	Agreed drop off time	
Child's name		
Child's age		
Location		

Special requirements

Custodian's details	
Name	
Relationship to child	
Address	
Email	
Tel. no.	
Signature	

Notes

Visit details			
Date			
Weekday			
Pick up time		Agreed pick up time	
Drop off time		Agreed drop off time	
Child's name			
Child's age			
Location			

Special requirements

Custodian's details	
Name	
Relationship to child	
Address	
Email	
Tel. no.	
Signature	

Notes

Visit details			
Date			
Weekday			
Pick up time		Agreed pick up time	
Drop off time		Agreed drop off time	
Child's name			
Child's age			
Location			

Special requirements

Custodian's details	
Name	
Relationship to child	
Address	
Email	
Tel. no.	
Signature	

Notes

Visit details			
Date			
Weekday			
Pick up time		Agreed pick up time	
Drop off time		Agreed drop off time	
Child's name			
Child's age			
Location			

Special requirements

Custodian's details	
Name	
Relationship to child	
Address	
Email	
Tel. no.	
Signature	

Notes

Visit details			
Date			
Weekday			
Pick up time		Agreed pick up time	
Drop off time		Agreed drop off time	
Child's name			
Child's age			
Location			

Special requirements

Custodian's details	
Name	
Relationship to child	
Address	
Email	
Tel. no.	
Signature	

Notes

Visit details		
Date		
Weekday		
Pick up time	Agreed pick up time	
Drop off time	Agreed drop off time	
Child's name		
Child's age		
Location		

Special requirements

Custodian's details	
Name	
Relationship to child	
Address	
Email	
Tel. no.	
Signature	

Notes

Visit details			
Date			
Weekday			
Pick up time		Agreed pick up time	
Drop off time		Agreed drop off time	
Child's name			
Child's age			
Location			

Special requirements

Custodian's details	
Name	
Relationship to child	
Address	
Email	
Tel. no.	
Signature	

Notes

Visit details			
Date			
Weekday			
Pick up time		Agreed pick up time	
Drop off time		Agreed drop off time	
Child's name			
Child's age			
Location			

Special requirements

Custodian's details	
Name	
Relationship to child	
Address	
Email	
Tel. no.	
Signature	

Notes

Visit details		
Date		
Weekday		
Pick up time	Agreed pick up time	
Drop off time	Agreed drop off time	
Child's name		
Child's age		
Location		

Special requirements

Custodian's details	
Name	
Relationship to child	
Address	
Email	
Tel. no.	
Signature	

Notes

Visit details		
Date		
Weekday		
Pick up time		Agreed pick up time	
Drop off time		Agreed drop off time	
Child's name		
Child's age		
Location		

Special requirements

Custodian's details	
Name	
Relationship to child	
Address	
Email	
Tel. no.	
Signature	

Notes

Visit details		
Date		
Weekday		
Pick up time	Agreed pick up time	
Drop off time	Agreed drop off time	
Child's name		
Child's age		
Location		

Special requirements

Custodian's details	
Name	
Relationship to child	
Address	
Email	
Tel. no.	
Signature	

Notes

Visit details			
Date			
Weekday			
Pick up time		Agreed pick up time	
Drop off time		Agreed drop off time	
Child's name			
Child's age			
Location			

Special requirements

Custodian's details	
Name	
Relationship to child	
Address	
Email	
Tel. no.	
Signature	

Notes

Visit details	
Date	
Weekday	
Pick up time	Agreed pick up time
Drop off time	Agreed drop off time
Child's name	
Child's age	
Location	

Special requirements

Custodian's details	
Name	
Relationship to child	
Address	
Email	
Tel. no.	
Signature	

Notes

Visit details			
Date			
Weekday			
Pick up time		Agreed pick up time	
Drop off time		Agreed drop off time	
Child's name			
Child's age			
Location			

Special requirements

Custodian's details	
Name	
Relationship to child	
Address	
Email	
Tel. no.	
Signature	

Notes

Visit details

Date	
Weekday	
Pick up time	Agreed pick up time	
Drop off time	Agreed drop off time	
Child's name	
Child's age	
Location	

Special requirements

Custodian's details

Name	
Relationship to child	
Address	
Email	
Tel. no.	
Signature	

Notes

Visit details			
Date			
Weekday			
Pick up time		Agreed pick up time	
Drop off time		Agreed drop off time	
Child's name			
Child's age			
Location			

Special requirements

Custodian's details	
Name	
Relationship to child	
Address	
Email	
Tel. no.	
Signature	

Notes

Visit details		
Date		
Weekday		
Pick up time		Agreed pick up time	
Drop off time		Agreed drop off time	
Child's name		
Child's age		
Location		

Special requirements

Custodian's details	
Name	
Relationship to child	
Address	
Email	
Tel. no.	
Signature	

Notes

Visit details			
Date			
Weekday			
Pick up time		Agreed pick up time	
Drop off time		Agreed drop off time	
Child's name			
Child's age			
Location			

Special requirements

Custodian's details	
Name	
Relationship to child	
Address	
Email	
Tel. no.	
Signature	

Notes

Visit details	
Date	
Weekday	

		Agreed pick up time	
Pick up time		Agreed pick up time	
Drop off time		Agreed drop off time	

Child's name	
Child's age	
Location	

Special requirements

Custodian's details	
Name	
Relationship to child	
Address	
Email	
Tel. no.	
Signature	

Notes

Visit details		
Date		
Weekday		
Pick up time	Agreed pick up time	
Drop off time	Agreed drop off time	
Child's name		
Child's age		
Location		

Special requirements

Custodian's details	
Name	
Relationship to child	
Address	
Email	
Tel. no.	
Signature	

Notes

Visit details			
Date			
Weekday			
Pick up time		Agreed pick up time	
Drop off time		Agreed drop off time	
Child's name			
Child's age			
Location			

Special requirements

Custodian's details	
Name	
Relationship to child	
Address	
Email	
Tel. no.	
Signature	

Notes

Visit details	
Date	
Weekday	
Pick up time	Agreed pick up time	
Drop off time	Agreed drop off time	
Child's name	
Child's age	
Location	

Special requirements

Custodian's details	
Name	
Relationship to child	
Address	
Email	
Tel. no.	
Signature	

Notes

Visit details		
Date		
Weekday		
Pick up time		Agreed pick up time
Drop off time		Agreed drop off time
Child's name		
Child's age		
Location		

Special requirements

Custodian's details	
Name	
Relationship to child	
Address	
Email	
Tel. no.	
Signature	

Notes

Visit details		
Date		
Weekday		
Pick up time	Agreed pick up time	
Drop off time	Agreed drop off time	
Child's name		
Child's age		
Location		

Special requirements

Custodian's details	
Name	
Relationship to child	
Address	
Email	
Tel. no.	
Signature	

Notes

Visit details		
Date		
Weekday		
Pick up time		Agreed pick up time
Drop off time		Agreed drop off time
Child's name		
Child's age		
Location		

Special requirements

Custodian's details	
Name	
Relationship to child	
Address	
Email	
Tel. no.	
Signature	

Notes

Visit details		
Date		
Weekday		
Pick up time	Agreed pick up time	
Drop off time	Agreed drop off time	
Child's name		
Child's age		
Location		

Special requirements

Custodian's details
Name	
Relationship to child	
Address	
Email	
Tel. no.	
Signature	

Notes

Visit details		
Date		
Weekday		
Pick up time	Agreed pick up time	
Drop off time	Agreed drop off time	
Child's name		
Child's age		
Location		

Special requirements

Custodian's details	
Name	
Relationship to child	
Address	
Email	
Tel. no.	
Signature	

Notes

Visit details			
Date			
Weekday			
Pick up time		Agreed pick up time	
Drop off time		Agreed drop off time	
Child's name			
Child's age			
Location			

Special requirements

Custodian's details	
Name	
Relationship to child	
Address	
Email	
Tel. no.	
Signature	

Notes

Visit details		
Date		
Weekday		
Pick up time		Agreed pick up time
Drop off time		Agreed drop off time
Child's name		
Child's age		
Location		

Special requirements

Custodian's details	
Name	
Relationship to child	
Address	
Email	
Tel. no.	
Signature	

Notes

Visit details			
Date			
Weekday			
Pick up time		Agreed pick up time	
Drop off time		Agreed drop off time	
Child's name			
Child's age			
Location			

Special requirements

Custodian's details	
Name	
Relationship to child	
Address	
Email	
Tel. no.	
Signature	

Notes

Visit details			
Date			
Weekday			
Pick up time		Agreed pick up time	
Drop off time		Agreed drop off time	
Child's name			
Child's age			
Location			

Special requirements

Custodian's details	
Name	
Relationship to child	
Address	
Email	
Tel. no.	
Signature	

Notes

Visit details		
Date		
Weekday		
Pick up time	Agreed pick up time	
Drop off time	Agreed drop off time	
Child's name		
Child's age		
Location		

Special requirements

Custodian's details	
Name	
Relationship to child	
Address	
Email	
Tel. no.	
Signature	

Notes

Visit details		
Date		
Weekday		
Pick up time	Agreed pick up time	
Drop off time	Agreed drop off time	
Child's name		
Child's age		
Location		

Special requirements

Custodian's details	
Name	
Relationship to child	
Address	
Email	
Tel. no.	
Signature	

Notes

Visit details			
Date			
Weekday			
Pick up time		Agreed pick up time	
Drop off time		Agreed drop off time	
Child's name			
Child's age			
Location			

Special requirements

Custodian's details	
Name	
Relationship to child	
Address	
Email	
Tel. no.	
Signature	

Notes

Visit details		
Date		
Weekday		
Pick up time	Agreed pick up time	
Drop off time	Agreed drop off time	
Child's name		
Child's age		
Location		

Special requirements

Custodian's details	
Name	
Relationship to child	
Address	
Email	
Tel. no.	
Signature	

Notes

Visit details

Date	
Weekday	
Pick up time	Agreed pick up time
Drop off time	Agreed drop off time
Child's name	
Child's age	
Location	

Special requirements

Custodian's details

Name	
Relationship to child	
Address	
Email	
Tel. no.	
Signature	

Notes

Visit details			
Date			
Weekday			
Pick up time		Agreed pick up time	
Drop off time		Agreed drop off time	
Child's name			
Child's age			
Location			

Special requirements

Custodian's details	
Name	
Relationship to child	
Address	
Email	
Tel. no.	
Signature	

Notes

Visit details			
Date			
Weekday			
Pick up time		Agreed pick up time	
Drop off time		Agreed drop off time	
Child's name			
Child's age			
Location			

Special requirements

Custodian's details	
Name	
Relationship to child	
Address	
Email	
Tel. no.	
Signature	

Notes

Visit details		
Date		
Weekday		
Pick up time		Agreed pick up time	
Drop off time		Agreed drop off time	
Child's name		
Child's age		
Location		

Special requirements

Custodian's details	
Name	
Relationship to child	
Address	
Email	
Tel. no.	
Signature	

Notes

Visit details			
Date			
Weekday			
Pick up time		Agreed pick up time	
Drop off time		Agreed drop off time	
Child's name			
Child's age			
Location			

Special requirements

Custodian's details	
Name	
Relationship to child	
Address	
Email	
Tel. no.	
Signature	

Notes

Visit details		
Date		
Weekday		
Pick up time		Agreed pick up time
Drop off time		Agreed drop off time
Child's name		
Child's age		
Location		

Special requirements

Custodian's details	
Name	
Relationship to child	
Address	
Email	
Tel. no.	
Signature	

Notes

Visit details			
Date			
Weekday			
Pick up time		Agreed pick up time	
Drop off time		Agreed drop off time	
Child's name			
Child's age			
Location			

Special requirements

Custodian's details	
Name	
Relationship to child	
Address	
Email	
Tel. no.	
Signature	

Notes

Visit details		
Date		
Weekday		
Pick up time	Agreed pick up time	
Drop off time	Agreed drop off time	
Child's name		
Child's age		
Location		

Special requirements

Custodian's details	
Name	
Relationship to child	
Address	
Email	
Tel. no.	
Signature	

Notes

Visit details			
Date			
Weekday			
Pick up time		Agreed pick up time	
Drop off time		Agreed drop off time	
Child's name			
Child's age			
Location			

Special requirements

Custodian's details	
Name	
Relationship to child	
Address	
Email	
Tel. no.	
Signature	

Notes

Visit details		
Date		
Weekday		
Pick up time	Agreed pick up time	
Drop off time	Agreed drop off time	
Child's name		
Child's age		
Location		

Special requirements

Custodian's details	
Name	
Relationship to child	
Address	
Email	
Tel. no.	
Signature	

Notes

Visit details	
Date	
Weekday	
Pick up time	Agreed pick up time	
Drop off time	Agreed drop off time	
Child's name	
Child's age	
Location	

Special requirements

Custodian's details	
Name	
Relationship to child	
Address	
Email	
Tel. no.	
Signature	

Notes

Made in the USA
Columbia, SC
28 February 2019